Leckie
the education publisher
for Scotland

Primary **Maths** for **Scotland**

1st Level Maths

1B

Practice Workbook 1

© 2024 Leckie

001/01082024

10 9 8 7 6 5 4 3 2 1

ISBN 9780008680299

Published by
Leckie
An imprint of HarperCollins Publishers
Westerhill Road, Bishopbriggs, Glasgow, G64 2QT

T: 0844 576 8126 F: 0844 576 8131
leckiescotland@harpercollins.co.uk www.leckiescotland.co.uk

HarperCollins Publishers
Macken House, 39/40 Mayor Street Upper, Dublin 1, D01 C9W8, Ireland

Publisher: Fiona McGlade

Special thanks
Project editor: Peter Dennis
Layout: Siliconchips
Proofreader: Julianna Dunn

A CIP Catalogue record for this book is available from the British Library.

Acknowledgements
Images © Shutterstock.com

Whilst every effort has been made to trace the copyright holders, in cases where this has been unsuccessful, or if any have inadvertently been overlooked, the Publishers would gladly receive any information enabling them to rectify any error or omission at the first opportunity.

Printed in India by Multivista Global Pvt. Ltd.

Contents

Answers
Check your answers to this workbook online: https://collins.co.uk/pages/scottish-primary-maths

1 Which is the closest ten to these numbers? Use the number line to help you. Circle the nearest ten.

a) 21

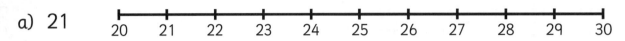

b) 37

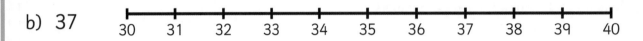

c) 44

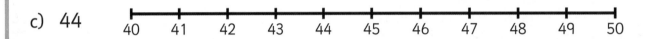

d) 76

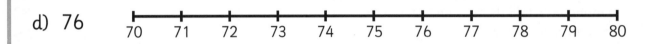

2 Isla is rounding numbers to the nearest ten. For each one, circle the tick or the cross to show if she is right or wrong. Use the number lines to help you.

a) 34 should be rounded up to 40.

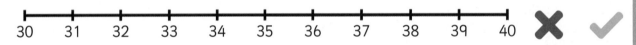

b) 88 should be rounded up to 90.

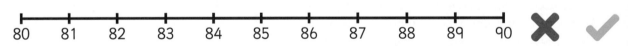

c) 14 should be rounded down to 10.

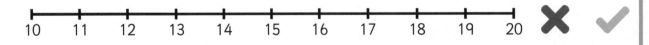

d) 58 should be rounded down to 50.

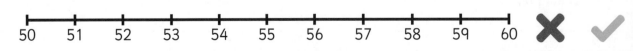

3 Nuria says that 85 rounded to the nearest ten is 90. Amman thinks that it is 80. Who is right? Explain your answer.

★ **Challenge**

1. Think of a two-digit number (for example, 67).

   a) Show this on a number line and where it sits between both tens.

   b) Circle the ten it is closer to.

2. Think of a three-digit number.

   a) Show this on a number line and where it sits between both tens.

   b) Circle the ten it is closer to.

1 Estimate the answer to these problems by rounding to the nearest ten. One has been done for you.

a) 16 + 12

16 rounded to the nearest 10 is 20 .

12 rounded to the nearest 10 is 10 .

20 + 10 = 30

so 16 + 12 is about 30 .

b) 9 + 19

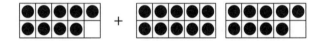

9 rounded to the nearest 10 is _____ .

19 rounded to the nearest 10 is _____ .

_____ + _____ = _____

so 9 + 19 is about _____ .

c) 28 + 14

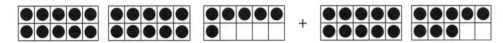

28 rounded to the nearest 10 is [ ].

14 rounded to the nearest 10 is [ ].

[ ] + [ ] = [ ]

so 28 + 14 is about [ ].

d) 26 + 18

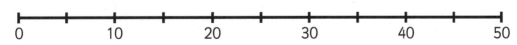

26 rounded to the nearest 10 is [ ].

18 rounded to the nearest 10 is [ ].

[ ] + [ ] = [ ]

so 26 + 18 is about [ ].

2 Estimate the answer to these problems by rounding to the nearest ten.

Use the number lines to help you.

a) 34 − 7 = is about 30 − 10 = 20

b) 27 − 18 is about [ ] − [ ] = [ ]

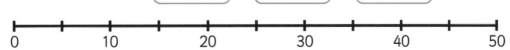

c) 36 − 12 is about [ ] − [ ] = [ ]

```
|----|----|----|----|----|----|----|----|----|----|
0         10        20        30        40        50
```

d) 46 − 19 is about [ ] − [ ] = [ ]

```
|----|----|----|----|----|----|----|----|----|----|
0         10        20        30        40        50
```

3 a) Isla has £51 and she wants to buy a game that costs £18.

I think I will have £30 left.

Is Isla correct? [YES]   [NO]

Show how you worked it out.

b) Finlay has £65 and he wants to buy a basketball that costs £29.

I think I will have £45 left.

Is Finlay correct? | YES | | NO |

Show how you worked it out.

★ **Challenge**

You have £78!

a) Think of an item to buy and decide how much it will cost (between £30 and £60).

b) Write your own word problem about your item.

c) Give your word problem to a partner to estimate the answer by rounding. Do you agree on the answer?

2.1 Reading and writing two-digit numbers

1 Use the 100 square below.

a) Colour number sixteen blue.

b) Colour number eighty-nine green.

c) Colour number sixty-six pink.

d) Colour number fifty yellow.

e) Colour number seventy-two purple.

f) Colour number ninety-four orange.

1	2	3	4	5	6	7	8	9	10
11	12	13	14	15	16	17	18	19	20
21	22	23	24	25	26	27	28	29	30
31	32	33	34	35	36	37	38	39	40
41	42	43	44	45	46	47	48	49	50
51	52	53	54	55	56	57	58	59	60
61	62	63	64	65	66	67	68	69	70
71	72	73	74	75	76	77	78	79	80
81	82	83	84	85	86	87	88	89	90
91	92	93	94	95	96	97	98	99	100

2 Write these numbers in words.

a) 79

b) 33

c) 85

d) 47

e) 61

3 Draw lines to match each race car to its number name. For example, 14 would match with fourteen.

55

19

27

38

nineteen

ninety-four

eighty-three

fifty-five

seventy-one

twenty-seven

forty

thirty-eight

40

71

83

94

⭐ **Challenge**

a) Write the number after 88 in numerals and in words.

b) Write the number before sixty-nine in numerals and in words.

c) Write the number after 73 in numerals and in words.

d) Write the number before ninety in numerals and in words.

2.2 Naming and ordering the hundreds

1 How many dots? Write each number in words and in numerals.

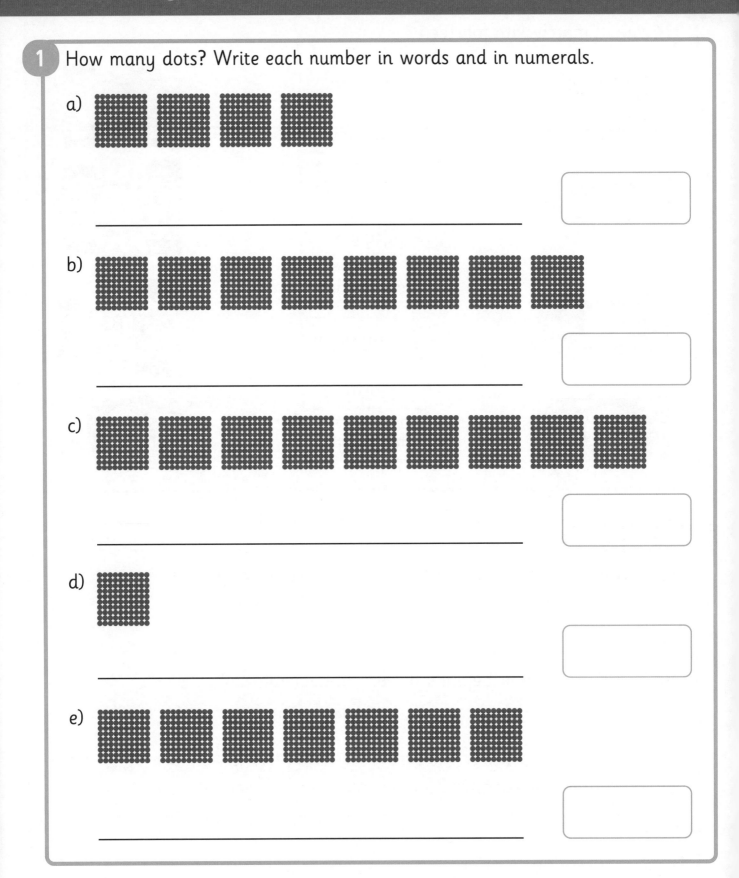

a)

_____

b)

_____

c)

_____

d)

_____

e)

_____

2 Write the missing numbers in numerals.

a) 100 sweets in each jar.

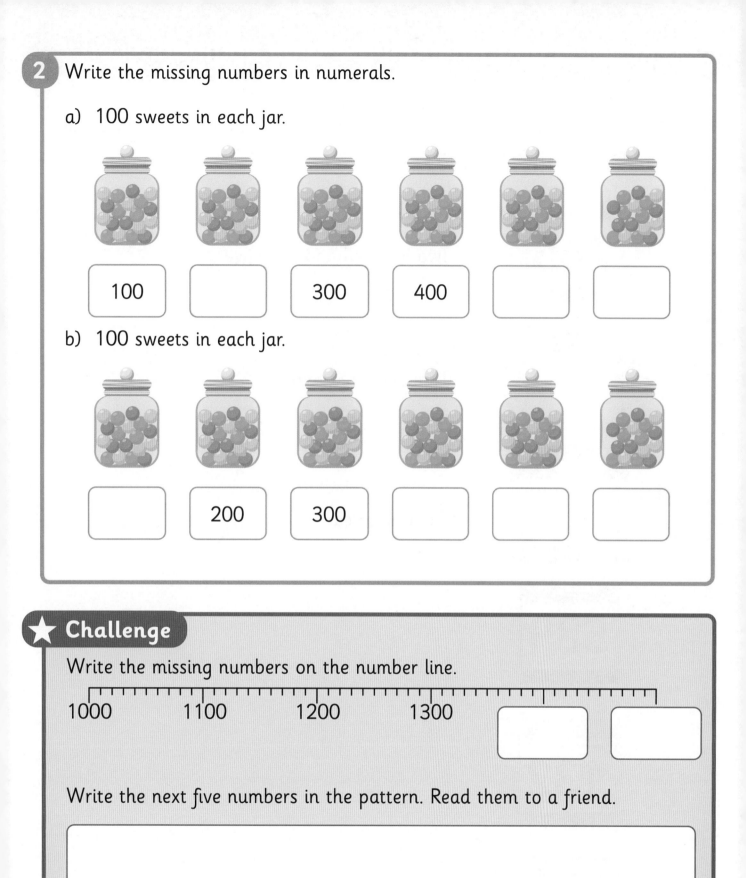

| 100 | | 300 | 400 | | |

b) 100 sweets in each jar.

| | 200 | 300 | | | |

★ **Challenge**

Write the missing numbers on the number line.

1000   1100   1200   1300

Write the next five numbers in the pattern. Read them to a friend.

2.3 Reading and writing three-digit numbers

1 Write the missing numerals or number words for each door. The first one has been done for you.

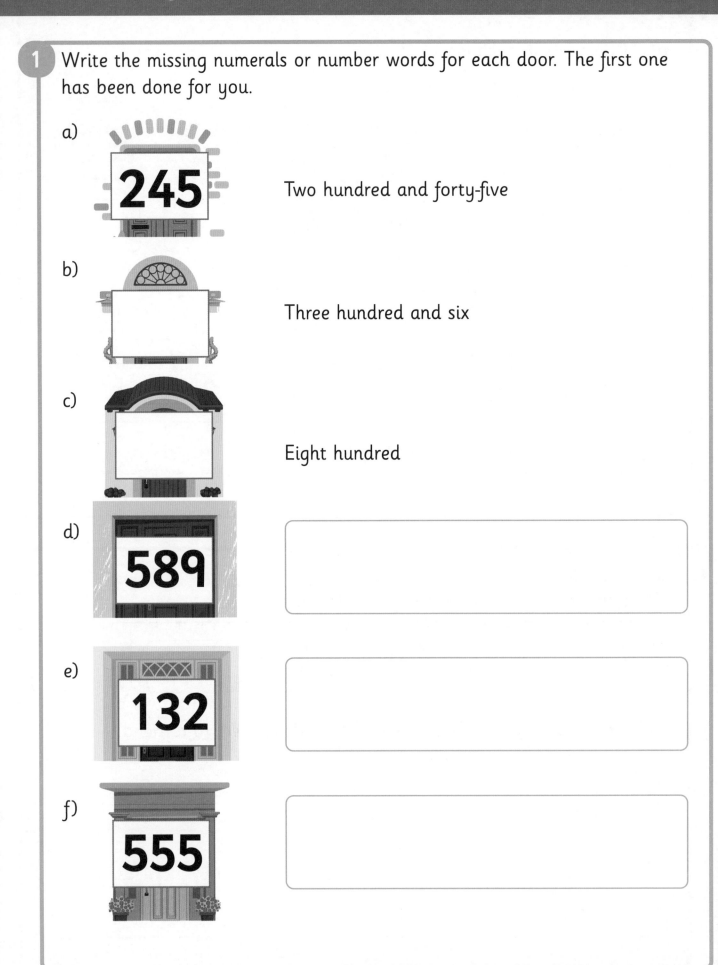

a) 245

Two hundred and forty-five

b)

Three hundred and six

c)

Eight hundred

d) 589

e) 132

f) 555

2

| 599 | 491 | 333 | 203 | 230 | 569 |

a) Finlay had ticket number four hundred and ninety-one. What did he win?

b) Amman had ticket number two hundred and three. What did he win?

c) Isla had ticket number three hundred and thirty-three. What did she win?

d) Nuria had ticket number five hundred and ninety-nine. What did she win?

e) Lola had ticket number five hundred and sixty-nine. What did she win?

f) Tony had ticket number two hundred and thirty. What did he win?

How many different three-digit numbers can you make with these number cards?

Write them in numerals and in words.

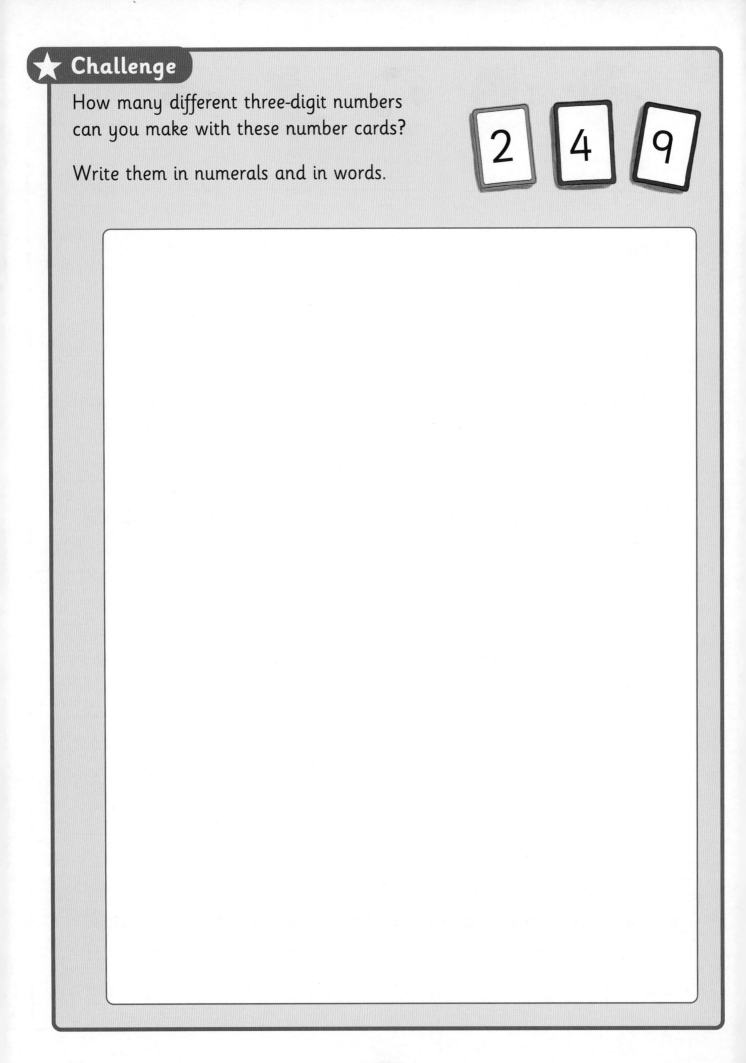

2.4 Counting forwards in ones

1 Write the missing numbers in numerals on the train carriages.

a)

| 128 | 129 | | |

b)

| 132 | 133 | | |

c)

| 467 | | 469 | |

d)

| 471 | | | 474 |

e)

| 697 | | 699 | |

e)

---

2 Write these numbers in words.

a) 555

b) 609

c) 340

d) 961

---

3 Isla has 367 pennies in her piggy bank. She counts five more pennies into her piggy bank one at a time. Say the next five numbers out loud then write them down in numerals and words.

a) Nuria has the number 654 on her raffle ticket.

Nuria has the next eight raffle tickets too.
Write down the numbers that she has.

b) Amman has the number 899 on his
raffle ticket.

Amman has the next eight raffle tickets
too. Write down the numbers that he has.

2.5 Counting backwards in ones

1 Count backwards in ones to fill in the missing numbers.

a) [ ] , [ ] , [ ] , [ ] , [ ] , 555

b) [ ] , [ ] , [ ] , [ ] , [ ] , 967

c) [ ] , [ ] , [ ] , [ ] , [ ] , 412

d) [ ] , [ ] , [ ] , [ ] , [ ] , 201

e) [ ] , [ ] , [ ] , [ ] , [ ] , 143

f) [ ] , [ ] , [ ] , [ ] , [ ] , 704

2 Count backwards in ones from the top of each ladder.

a) **709**

b) **345**

c) **987**

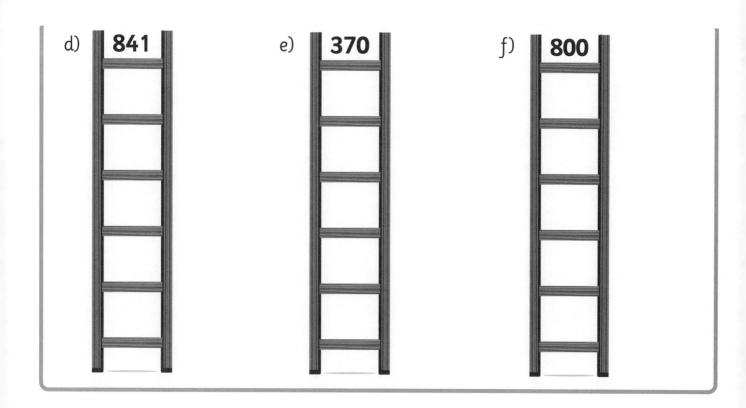

d) 841

e) 370

f) 800

3 Isla is counting backwards as she goes down the stairs.

a) Fill in the missing numbers.

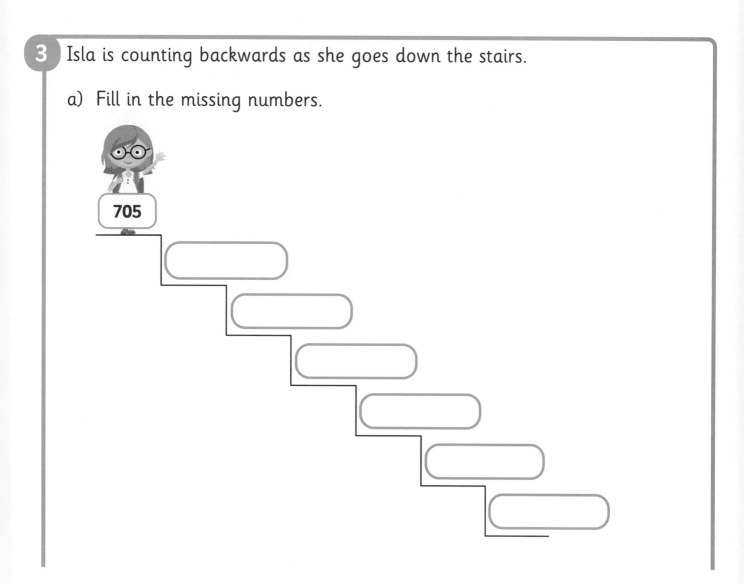

705

b) Fill in the missing numbers.

105

c) Fill in the missing numbers.

505

d) What do you notice?

★ **Challenge**

Finlay and Nuria are counting backwards in ones from 303. Write down the numbers they say on the number line. What do you notice?

						303

I think the same digit changes every time when you count backwards in ones.

I think the tens digit changes every time.

Who is correct, Finlay or Nuria?

2.6 Before, after and in between

1 Write the number that comes after:

a) 123 ☐   b) 356 ☐   c) 104 ☐

d) 709 ☐   e) 600 ☐   f) 899 ☐

2 Write the number that comes before:

a) 672 ☐   b) 349 ☐   c) 234 ☐

d) 401 ☐   e) 500 ☐   f) 899 ☐

3 Write the numbers that come in between:

a) 397, ☐ , ☐ , ☐ , ☐ , ☐ ,

☐ , ☐ , ☐ , ☐ , 407

b) 500, ☐ , ☐ , ☐ , ☐ , ☐ ,

☐ , ☐ , ☐ , ☐ , 510

c) 444, ☐ , ☐ , ☐ , ☐ , ☐ ,

☐ , ☐ , ☐ , ☐ , 454

d) 911, ☐ , ☐ , ☐ , ☐ , ☐ ,

☐ , ☐ , ☐ , ☐ , 921

4 Complete the following number sequences.

a) 345, ☐ , 347, 348, ☐ , ☐ , 351, ☐

b) 609, ☐ , ☐ , 612, ☐ , ☐ , ☐ , 616

c) ☐ , 456, 457, ☐ , ☐ , 460, ☐ , ☐ ,

★ **Challenge**

a) Make any three-digit number.

☐

b) Write down the number that comes before your number.

☐

c) Write the number that comes after your number.

☐

d) Write any 3 numbers that come in between 345 and 355.

☐ ☐ ☐

1 Write the number that is 10 more than:

a) 404

b) 678

c) 311

d) 888

e) 700

f) 501

2 Write the number that is 100 more than:

a) 403

b) 876

c) 580

d) 304

e) 799

f) 255

3 Count forwards in tens and then write in the numbers to complete each number pattern.

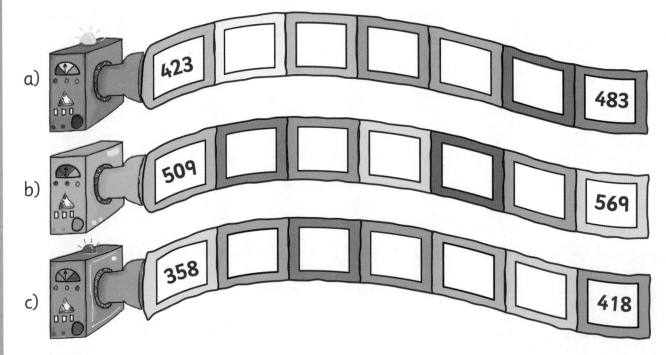

a) 423 | | | | | | 483

b) 509 | | | | | | 569

c) 358 | | | | | | 418

4 Count forwards in hundreds to complete each number pattern.

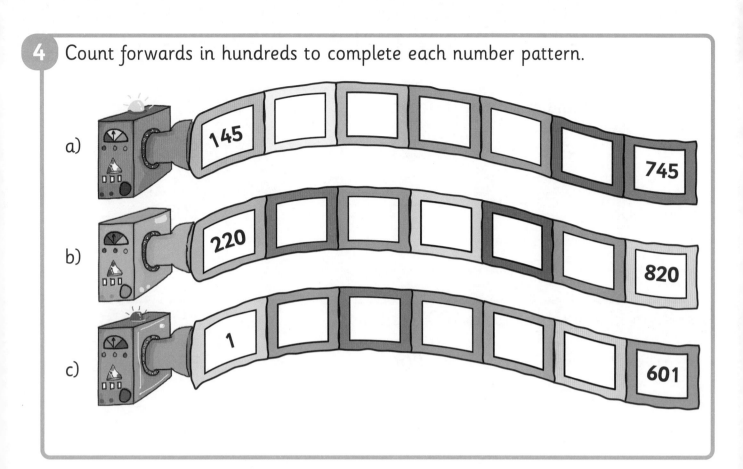

a) 145 ☐ ☐ ☐ ☐ ☐ 745

b) 220 ☐ ☐ ☐ ☐ ☐ 820

c) 1 ☐ ☐ ☐ ☐ ☐ 601

★ Challenge

Isla counted forwards in tens from 255 and so did Nuria.

Who is correct? Tick the correct person.

 255, 265, 275, 285, 295, 395, 495, 595 ☐

 255, 265, 275, 285, 295, 305, 315, 325 ☐

Choose your own three-digit number. Count forwards in tens. How far can you go?

2.8 Counting backwards in tens and hundreds

1 Write the number that is 10 less than:

a) 489 ☐   b) 321 ☐   c) 800 ☐

d) 608 ☐   e) 550 ☐   f) 505 ☐

2 Write the number that is 100 less than:

a) 467 ☐   b) 804 ☐   c) 590 ☐

d) 300 ☐   e) 712 ☐   f) 169 ☐

3 Work out the patterns to count backwards down the ladders.

a)

783
773

b)

945
845

c)

808
708

d)

135
125

a) Write down a three-digit number. Make each digit different.

b) Write the number that is one less than your number.

c) What is ten less than your number?

d) What is 100 less than your number?

Repeat this challenge for different three-digit numbers.

1 a) Finlay wants to put two marshmallows on top of each hot chocolate. How many marshmallows will he need?

b) Isla puts five sweets in each jar. How many sweets does Isla have?

c) How much money does Amman have?

2 Count backwards in twos. Write the correct number in the empty boxes.

a) 84, 82, [ ] , [ ] , [ ] , [ ]

b) 90, 88, [ ] , [ ] , [ ] , [ ]

c) 72, [ ] , [ ] , 66, [ ]

d) [ ] , [ ] , 44, [ ] , [ ]

3 Count backwards in fives. Write the correct number in the empty boxes.

a) 95, 90, [ ] , [ ] , [ ] , [ ]

b) 70, [ ] , [ ] , [ ] , [ ]

c) [ ] , 20, [ ] , 10, [ ]

d) [ ] , [ ] , [ ] , [ ] 45

★ **Challenge**

Find the missing numbers on the number lines.

a)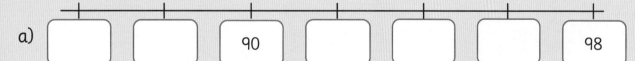

b)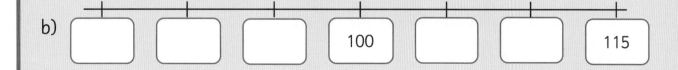

2.10 Counting in hundreds, tens and ones

1 Count in hundreds, tens and ones. How many dots are there in each question?

a)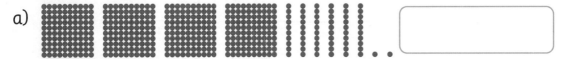

b)

c)

d)

e)

f)

2 Count in hundreds, tens and ones. How many blocks are there in each question?

a)

b)

c)

d)

Draw your own models using dots or blocks to show:

a) 249   b) 603   c) 140

1 Write the number shown by each set of base 10 blocks in two different ways. One has been done for you.

a)

Fifty-four = 50 + 4

b)

c)

d)

e)

2 Match each number to the correct number sentence.

60   30 + 2

            90 + 9   45

32   60 + 0

            40 + 5   78

99   70 + 8

3 How many different two-digit numbers can you make using these arrow cards?

4 0	1
6 0	6
9 0	8

★ Challenge

Finlay partitions the number 25 in two different ways.

Partition these numbers in different ways:

> 25 = 20 + 5.
> It can also be 10 + 15.

a) 31

b) 68

c) 99

1 For each pair of numbers show them on a number line and ✓ who has the greatest number.

a)

35   53   ✓

|30____35____40____45____50____55____60|
        ↑   ↑

b)

68   86

|60____70____80____90|

c)

42   24

|20____30____40____50|

d)

657   576

|570 580 590 600 610 620 630 640 650 660 670|

e)

507   517

|500____510____520____530|

2

| is greater than | is equal to | is less than |

Choose the correct phrases to complete the number chains.

a) 631 [ ] 531 [ ] 163

b) 809 [ ] 809 [ ] 709

c) 413 [ ] 341 [ ] 341

d) 45 [ ] 450 [ ] 673

★ **Challenge**

Write a three-digit number of your choice. [ ]

Can you create five different numbers using the same three digits?

[ ]

How many different numbers are possible if two digits are the same? Try it!

[ ]

What if all three digits are the same?

[ ]

1 These books should be in number order from smallest to largest but some are in the wrong place. Write the correct order under each set of books.

a)

34	39	37	40

b)

67	64	70	75

c)

95	80	85	91

d)

350	259	452	163

e)

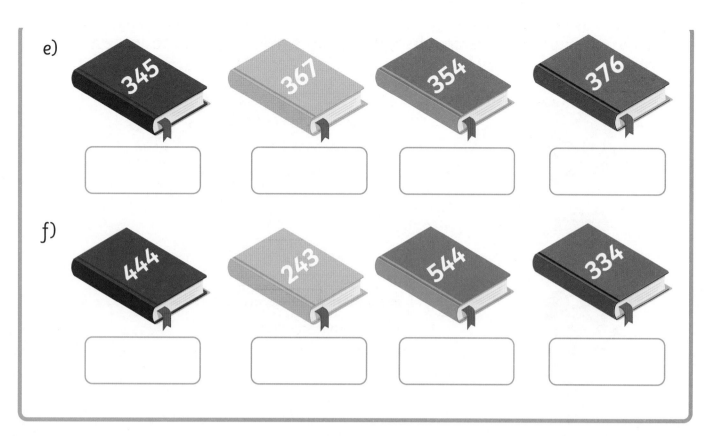

345   367   354   376

f)

444   243   544   334

2 Write these numbers in order from largest to smallest.

a) 8, 888, 808, 818, 878

b) 507, 500, 576, 501, 509

c) 401, 181, 326, 491, 321

d) 958, 458, 999, 499, 951

3 Isla and Nuria have ordered some numbers from smallest to largest. Tick the person you think is correct.

I think these numbers are ordered correctly from smallest to largest:
501, 510, 500, 505, 515, 550.

I think these numbers are ordered correctly from smallest to largest:
500, 501, 505, 510, 515, 550.

★ Challenge

Ask a friend to write ten three-digit numbers for you. Ask them to make sure they are not in order!

Now you order them in this box, from largest to smallest.

2.14 Ordinal numbers

1   Tony is first in the line when the bell rings.

| Laura | Wendy | Lola | Logan | Avie | Lucy | Olivia | Joe | Archer | Maggie | Finlay | Tony |

In what position are the children?

Write your answers in numerals and in words.

a)   Joe.

b)   Lucy.

c)   Logan.

d)   Laura.

e)   Olivia.

f)   Archer.

g)   The person in front of Avie.

h)   The person three behind Olivia.

2 Look at Olivia's diary.

February						
Sunday	Monday	Tuesday	Wednesday	Thursday	Friday	Saturday
				1 Shopping with Lucy	2	3
4	5	6	7 Cinema	8	9	10
11	12	13	14 Olivia's birthday	15	16	17
18 Dentist	19	20 School trip	21 Jude's Birthday / Amber sleepover	22	23	24 Lunch with Granddad
25	26	27	28			

a) When is Olivia's birthday?

b) Where is Olivia going on 7th February?

c) What is she doing on 18th February?

d) Who is she seeing on 24th February?

e) Where is she going on 20th February?

f) What is she doing on 1st February?

g) Whose birthday is on 21st February?

h) Where is she going on 21st February?

99th   1st   20th

5th   100th

2nd   30th

3rd

Sort these ordinal numbers from first to last.

Now write each ordinal number in words.

1 Use number buddies to 10 to help you work out each total. Show your working and the number buddies you used. One has been done for you.

a) $8 + 4 + 6 =$ ┌── 10 ──┐ over 4 + 6, box: $10 + 8 = 18$

b) $4 + 8 + 6 =$ [   ]

c) $8 + 4 + 2 =$ [   ]

d) $3 + 1 + 7 =$ [   ]

2 Match up the number buddies and then write the total.

One has been done for you.

a) $1 + 5 + 5 + 9 =$ [20]

b) $8 + 6 + 2 + 4 =$ [   ]

c) $9 + 7 + 1 + 3 =$ [   ]

d) $10 + 5 + 0 + 5 =$ [   ]

e) $7 + 4 + 6 + 3 =$ [   ]

f) $2 + 3 + 7 + 8 =$ [   ]

3 Which numbers are missing?

a) $8 + 6 + \boxed{} + 4 = 20$

b) $9 + 7 + 1 + 3 = \boxed{}$

c) $10 + 5 + \boxed{} + 5 = 20$

d) $\boxed{} + 4 + 6 + 3 = 20$

e) $1 + \boxed{} + 9 + 2 = 20$

f) $2 + 9 + 1 + \boxed{} = 20$

★ **Challenge**

How many different ways can you make 19 using:

a) three numbers?

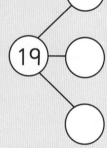

b) four numbers?

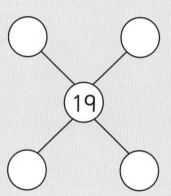

3.2 Doubles and near doubles

1 Use double facts to work out each near double.

a) 4 + 5 = double [ ] plus one = [ ] + 1 = [ ]

b) 5 + 6 = double [ ] plus one = [ ] + 1 = [ ]

c) 9 + 10 = double [ ] plus one = [ ] + 1 = [ ]

d) 8 + 9 = double [ ] plus one = [ ] + 1 = [ ]

e) 6 + 7 = double [ ] plus one = [ ] + 1 = [ ]

f) 7 + 8 = double [ ] plus one = [ ] + 1 = [ ]

2 The numbers around the outside of each triangle add up to 18.

Find the missing double fact then write the number sentence.

The first one has been done for you.

a)

8

18

8   2

2 + 8 + 8 = 18

b)

18

6

c)

4

18

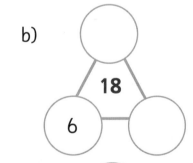

d)

0

18

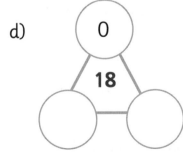

3 Match each problem to the double fact that can help you solve it, then find the answer.

a) 8 + 9 =    5 + 5

b) 7 + 8 =   8 + 8

c) 9 + 10 =   7 + 7

d) 6 + 5 =   9 + 9

★ **Challenge**

a) Isla has 7 blue flowers and 8 red flowers. How many flowers does she have? Can you use a double fact to work out your answer?

b) Can you think of your own number problem using a near double? Write one down and ask a friend to solve it.

3.3 Fact families

1 Write three different number sentences to complete each fact family. The first one has been done for you.

a) 6 + 14 = 20 | 14 + 6 = 20 | 20 − 6 = 14 | 20 − 14 = 6 |

b) 8 + 7 = 15

c) 11 + 6 = 17

d) 5 + 15 = 20

e) 8 + 9 = 17

f) 8 + 11 = 19

2 Isla writes a fact family for this **bar model.**

11 + 6 = 17   6 + 11 = 17

17 − 11 = 6   17 − 6 = 11

Write a fact family for each bar model.

a)

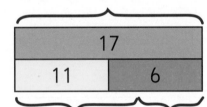

b)

18	
11	7

c)

12	
2	10

d)

16	
4	12

3 Find the missing numbers. You could use cubes or draw a bar model to help you.

a) [ ] + 12 = 15

b) 16 – [ ] = 9

c) [ ] – 9 = 7

d) [ ] + 9 = 18

Use these digits to make addition and subtraction number sentences.

How many different number sentences can you find?

| 7 | 4 | 9 | 15 | 8 | 13 | 11 | 16 |

3.4 Complements to the next multiple of 10

1 Use the number lines to count on to the next multiple of 10. Complete the number sentence.

a) 64

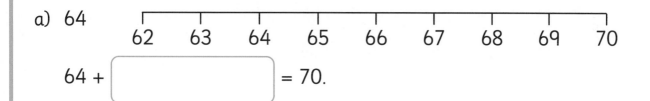

64 + [ ] = 70.

b) 44

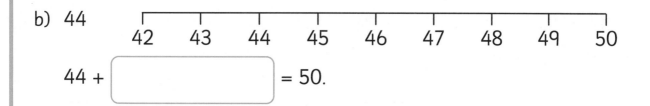

44 + [ ] = 50.

c) 72

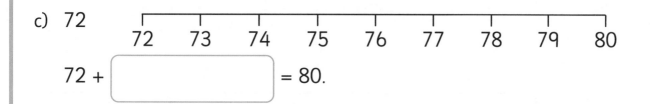

72 + [ ] = 80.

d) 32

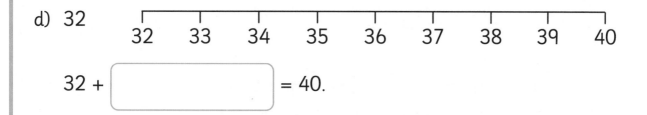

32 + [ ] = 40.

e) 93

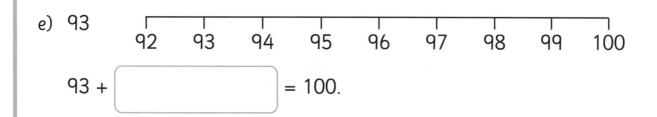

93 + [ ] = 100.

2 Use the number lines to count back to the next multiple of 10.
Complete the number sentence.

a) 55   47   48   49   50   51   52   53   54   55

55 – ☐ = 50.

b) 87   79   80   81   82   83   84   85   86   87

87 – ☐ = 80.

c) 76   68   69   70   71   72   73   74   75   76

76 – ☐ = 70.

d) 63   55   56   57   58   59   60   61   62   63

63 – ☐ = 60.

e) 48   40   41   42   43   44   45   46   47   48

48 – ☐ = 40.

f) 38   30   31   32   33   34   35   36   37   38

38 – ☐ = 30.

Write a multiple of 10 in each box to make the number sentences true.
How many different ways can you find?

a) 8 + ⬚ + ⬚ = 88

b) 76 − ⬚ − ⬚ = 6

c) 4 + ⬚ + ⬚ = 74

d) 61 − ⬚ − ⬚ = 1

1

a) $67 + 0 = $ ⬚ $67 + 1 = $ ⬚ $67 + 10 = $ ⬚

b) $31 + 0 = $ ⬚ $31 + 1 = $ ⬚ $31 + 10 = $ ⬚

c) ⬚ $+ 0 = 53$ ⬚ $+ 1 = 54$ ⬚ $+ 10 = 63$

d) ⬚ $+ 0 = 89$ ⬚ $+ 1 = 90$ ⬚ $+ 10 = 99$

e) $45 + $ ⬚ $= 45$ $45 + $ ⬚ $= 46$ $45 + $ ⬚ $= 55$

f) $76 + $ ⬚ $= 76$ ⬚ $+ 1 = 77$ $76 + 10 = $ ⬚

g) $92 + 0 = $ ⬚ $92 + $ ⬚ $= 93$ ⬚ $+ 10 = 93$

2 Use your answers to Question 1 to help you solve these number problems. Write down the calculation from Question 1 that helped you.

a) $45 + 11 = $ ⬚

b) $67 + 11 = $ ⬚

c) $89 + 11 = $ ⬚

d) $31 + 11 = $ ⬚

e) $53 + 11 = $ ⬚

f) $76 + 11 = $ ⬚

3 Find the missing numbers for each function machine.

a)

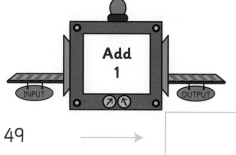

49 → [ ]

[ ] → 135

309 → [ ]

[ ] → 480

[ ] → 301

b)

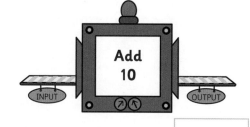

68 → [ ]

[ ] → 99

302 → [ ]

[ ] → 298

666 → [ ]

 **Challenge**

Nuria is working out the answer to 85 + 9. She **adds 10** to reach **95**. Then she **subtracts 1** to reach 94.

85 + 9 = 94

Add 9 to the number on each card.

| 67 | 85 | 32 | 71 | 90 |

3.6 Subtracting 0, 1 and 10

1 Write your answers in the boxes. Talk with a friend about what you notice.

a) 96 – 10 = ☐

86 – 10 = ☐

76 – 10 = ☐

66 – 10 = ☐

56 – 10 = ☐

46 – 10 = ☐

b) 71 – 1 = ☐

61 – 1 = ☐

51 – 1 = ☐

41 – 1 = ☐

31 – 1 = ☐

21 – 1 = ☐

c) 55 – 0 = ☐

45 – 0 = ☐

35 – 0 = ☐

25 – 0 = ☐

15 – 0 = ☐

5 – 0 = ☐

2 Use the missing numbers for each function machine.

a)

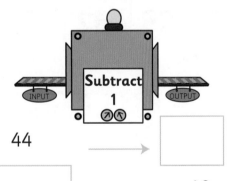

44 → ☐

☐ → 60

808 → ☐

☐ → 800

☐ → 410

b)

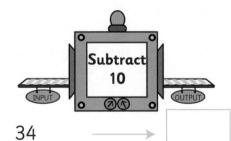

34 → ☐

☐ → 54

567 → ☐

☐ → 726

☐ → 900

3

a) $100 - 1 = \boxed{}$

b) $\boxed{} = 88 - 0$

c) $67 - \boxed{} = 57$

d) $32 - \boxed{} = 31$

e) $\boxed{} - 0 = 74$

f) $\boxed{} - 10 = 95$

★ **Challenge**

a) Write down three two-digit numbers.

b) Subtract 10 from each number.

c) Now subtract 11 from each new number.

d) What do you notice?

3.7 Adding and subtracting single- and double-digit numbers

1 Complete each number pattern. Write the next number sentence for each pattern.

a)
$$6 + 3 = \boxed{}$$
$$16 + 3 = \boxed{}$$
$$26 + 3 = \boxed{}$$
$$\boxed{} + \boxed{} = \boxed{}$$

b)
$$2 + 4 = \boxed{}$$
$$12 + 4 = \boxed{}$$
$$22 + 4 = \boxed{}$$
$$\boxed{} + \boxed{} = \boxed{}$$

c)
$$8 - 5 = \boxed{}$$
$$18 - 5 = \boxed{}$$
$$28 - 5 = \boxed{}$$
$$\boxed{} - \boxed{} = \boxed{}$$

d)
$$10 - 9 = \boxed{}$$
$$20 - 9 = \boxed{}$$
$$30 - 9 = \boxed{}$$
$$\boxed{} - \boxed{} = \boxed{}$$

2 Use the addition and subtraction facts you know to work out:

a)
$$4 + 4 = \boxed{}$$
$$34 + 4 = \boxed{}$$
$$94 + 4 = \boxed{}$$

b)
$$3 + 6 = \boxed{}$$
$$23 + 6 = \boxed{}$$
$$53 + 6 = \boxed{}$$

c)
$$5 + 2 = \boxed{}$$
$$65 + 2 = \boxed{}$$
$$85 + 2 = \boxed{}$$

d)
$$8 - 3 = \boxed{}$$
$$58 - 3 = \boxed{}$$
$$98 - 3 = \boxed{}$$

e)
$$9 - 7 = \boxed{}$$
$$39 - 7 = \boxed{}$$
$$89 - 7 = \boxed{}$$

f)
$$6 - 5 = \boxed{}$$
$$46 - 5 = \boxed{}$$
$$76 - 5 = \boxed{}$$

3 Complete these calculations. Write the known fact you used to help you.

For example: 5 + 32 = 37   Known fact: 5 + 2 = 7

a) 7 + 62 = [____]

b) 7 + [____] = 69

c) 4 + 62 = [____]

d) 95 – 5 = [____]

e) 98 – [____] = 58

[____] + [____] = [____]

[____] + [____] = [____]

[____] + [____] = [____]

[____] – [____] = [____]

[____] – [____] = [____]

★ Challenge

I am thinking of a number. When I add 5 to it I get 48. What number did I start with?

[____]

Amman starts with his answer. First, he subtracts 8, then adds 4, then takes away 2. Write down Amman's new number. Show your working.

[____]

Now try Amman's subtract 8, add 4, take away 2 rule for two different two-digit numbers. Tell a friend what you notice.

[____]

3.8 Adding and subtracting multiples of 10 to and from two-digit numbers

1 Use known facts to help you find the answers.

Write the known fact you used.

For example: $50 + 20 = 70$ Known fact: $5 + 2 = 7$

a) $30 + 60 =$ [   ]   [   ] $+$ [   ] $=$ [   ]

b) $20 + 40 =$ [   ]   [   ] $+$ [   ] $=$ [   ]

c) $90 - 30 =$ [   ]   [   ] $-$ [   ] $=$ [   ]

d) $60 - 50 =$ [   ]   [   ] $-$ [   ] $=$ [   ]

e) $20 + 80 =$ [   ]   [   ] $+$ [   ] $=$ [   ]

f) $100 - 90 =$ [   ]   [   ] $-$ [   ] $=$ [   ]

2 Count on or back in tens to work out each answer.

Use the number lines to help you.

a) 30 + 80 = ☐

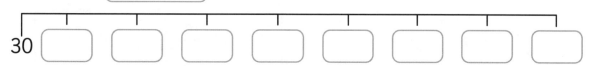

b) 70 + 50 = ☐

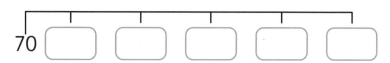

c) 90 + 80 = ☐

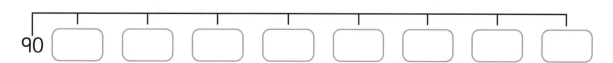

d) 120 − 40 = ☐

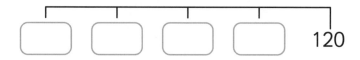

e) 190 − 70 = ☐

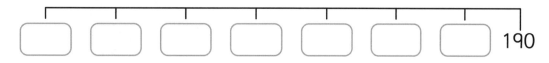

f) 170 − 90 = ☐

3 Complete these addition puzzles.

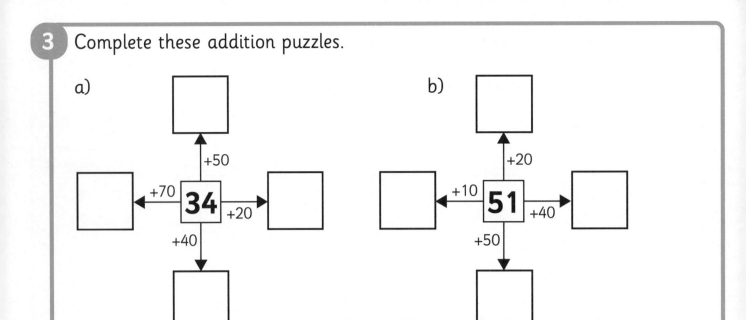

a)

+50
+70 **34** +20
+40

b)

+20
+10 **51** +40
+50

4 Complete these subtraction puzzles.

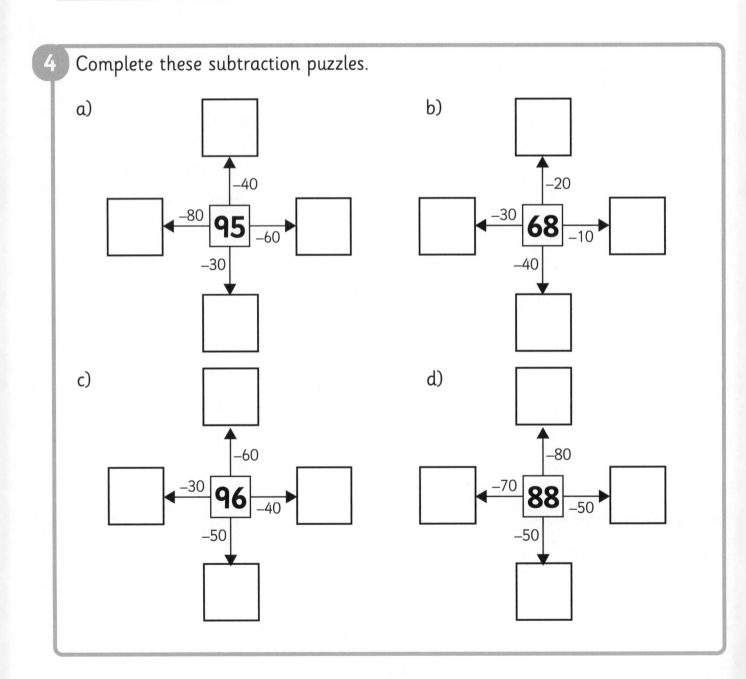

a)

−40
−80 **95** −60
−30

b)

−20
−30 **68** −10
−40

c)

−60
−30 **96** −40
−50

d)

−80
−70 **88** −50
−50

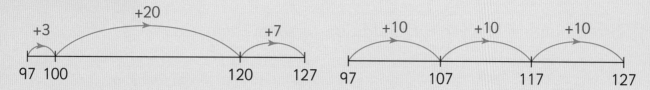

Both number lines show that 97 + 30 = 127.

a) Draw two different number lines to show 567 + 60 =

b) Draw two different number lines to show 834 − 40 =

1 Use a number line for each addition to solve them.

a)

44 + 6 =

b)

87 + 4 =

c)

35 + 7 =

d)

99 + 9 =

2 Use a number line for each subtraction to solve them.

a)

74 – 7 =

b)

41 – 9 =

c)

55 – 6 =

d)

101 – 8 =

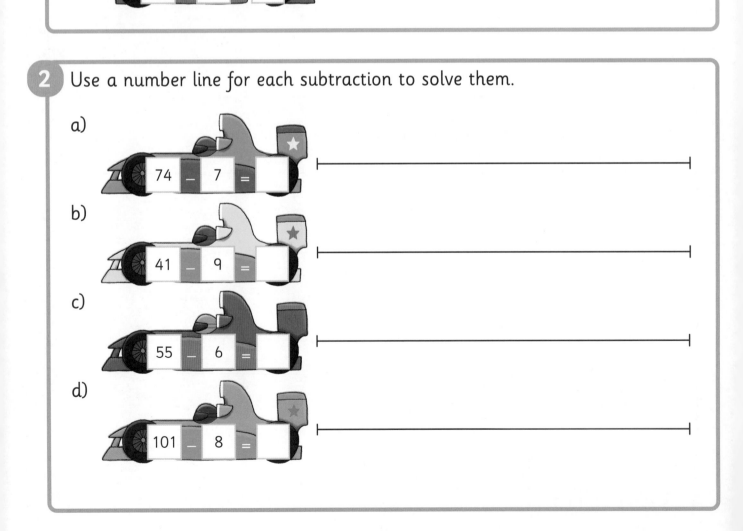

3 Use a number line to solve each calculation.

a) $96 + \boxed{} = 103$

b) $83 = 75 + \boxed{}$

c) $76 - \boxed{} = 68$

d) $48 = 56 - \boxed{}$

e) $57 + \boxed{} = 66$

f) $66 = 58 + \boxed{}$

Write three subtraction number sentences with the numbers below as your answers. You may only subtract numbers that are greater than 3 and less than 10. The first one has been done for you.

a) 27

35 − 8 = 27   31 − 4 = 27   32 − 5 = 27

b) 34

c) 66

d) 71

e) 85

3.10 Adding two-digit numbers

1 Find each total. Show how you worked your answers out on the empty number lines.

a) 26 + 54 = ⬚ ├─────────────────────────────────┤

b) 38 + 49 = ⬚ ├─────────────────────────────────┤

c) 35 + 46 = ⬚ ├─────────────────────────────────┤

d) 25 + 77 = ⬚ ├─────────────────────────────────┤

e) 38 + 87 = ⬚ ├─────────────────────────────────┤

f) 47 + 75 = ⬚ ├─────────────────────────────────┤

2 Fill in the missing numbers on each number line, then write the addition number sentence.

a)
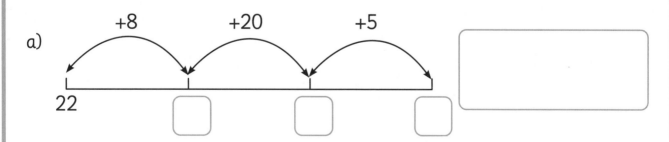

b)

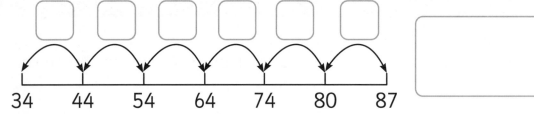

34   44   54   64   74   80   87

c)

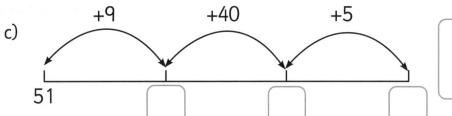

51

d)

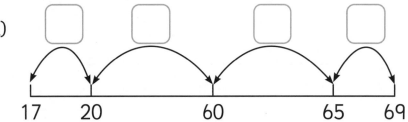

17   20   60   65   69

---

3 Partition both numbers to work out each answer. One has been done for you.

a)
36 + 42

30 + 40 = 70

6 + 2 = 8

70 + 8 = 78

b)
71 + 27

c)
29 + 71

d)
58 + 15

e)
67 + 24

f)
21 + 79

Use a number line to work out each answer. Compare your method with a partner.

a) [   ] + 48 = 95

b) 23 + [   ] = 81

c) [   ] + 53 = 81

d) 38 + [   ] = 95

3.11 Subtracting two-digit numbers

 Find each difference. Show how you worked your answers out on the empty number lines.

a)

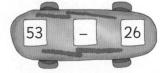

53 – 26 = ⬜ ├───┤

b)

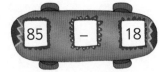

85 – 18 = ⬜ ├───┤

c)

75 – 49 = ⬜ ├───┤

d)

64 – 37 = ⬜ ├───┤

e)

96 – 47 = ⬜ ├───┤

f)

81 – 28 = ⬜ ├───┤

2 Fill in the missing numbers on each number line, then write the subtraction number sentence.

a)

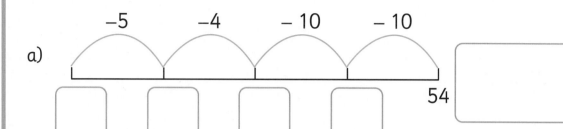

-5 -4 -10 -10

[ ] [ ] [ ] [ ]   54

b)

[ ] [ ] [ ] [ ]

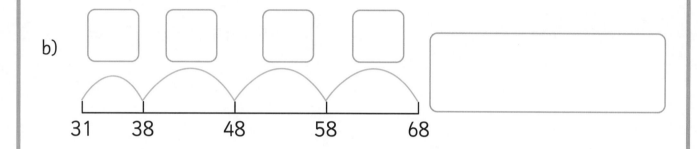

31   38   48   58   68

c)

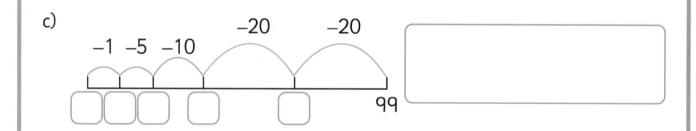

-1 -5 -10 -20 -20

[ ] [ ] [ ] [ ]   [ ]   99

d)

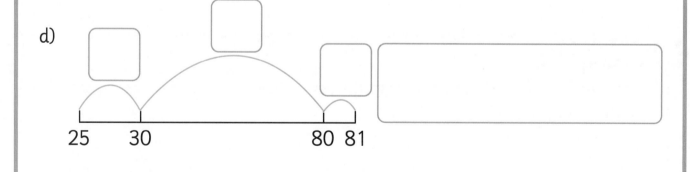

25   30   80 81

3 Partition both numbers to work out the answers to these subtractions. The first one has been done for you.

a)
67 – 23

60 – 20 = 40

7 – 3 = 4

40 + 4 = 44

b)
77 – 25

c)
99 – 71

d)
55 – 15

e)
78 – 42

f)
89 – 53

 Challenge

Draw empty number lines to help you solve these problems. Compare your method with a partner.

a) 96 – ☐ = 29 |———————————————————|

b) ☐ – 37 = 34 |———————————————————|

3.12 Inverse relationships

1 Use an empty number line to solve each subtraction. Check each answer by counting on.

a) $79 - 26 = \boxed{}$ $\qquad$ $26 + \boxed{} = 79$

b) $85 - 44 = \boxed{}$ $\qquad$ $44 + \boxed{} = 85$

c) $66 - 38 = \boxed{}$ $\qquad$ $38 + \boxed{} = 66$

d) $80 - 53 = \boxed{}$ $\qquad$ $53 + \boxed{} = 80$

2 Write one subtraction fact and one addition fact for each number line.

a)
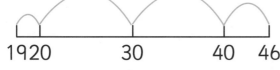
19 20   30   40   46

$46 - \boxed{} = 19$ $\qquad$ $19 + \boxed{} = 46$

b)
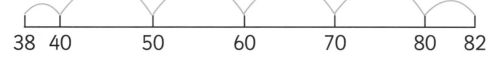
38   40   50   60   70   80   82

$82 - \boxed{} = 38$ $\qquad$ $38 + \boxed{} = 82$

c)
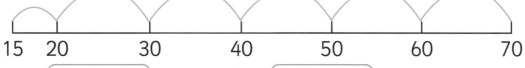
15   20   30   40   50   60   70

$70 - \boxed{} = 15$ $\qquad$ $15 + \boxed{} = 70$

3 Complete each number sentence by counting on or counting back.
Show your working.

a) $90 = 66 + \boxed{}$

|——————————————————————————————————|

b) $78 = \boxed{} + 25$

|——————————————————————————————————|

c) $\boxed{} + 36 = 78$

|——————————————————————————————————|

d) $88 - \boxed{} = 56$

|——————————————————————————————————|

e) $76 = \boxed{} - 53$

|——————————————————————————————————|

f) $97 = 53 + \boxed{}$

|——————————————————————————————————|

Use these number cards to make addition and subtraction number sentences. How many can you find?

65   **16**   **49**

1 Look at the numbers in this table.

6	3	5
9	7	1
8	9	3

a) Put a tick next to the horizontal line that totals 20.

b) Colour the vertical line that makes the biggest total in yellow.

c) Colour the vertical line that makes the smallest total in blue.

2 Look at the numbers in this table.

6	9	4	6
7	5	10	8
5	8	9	7

a) Put a tick next to the horizontal line that totals 30.

b) Colour the horizontal line that totals 29 in yellow.

c) Colour the vertical line that makes the smallest total in blue.

3 Look at the numbers in this table.

11	16	12	9
15	8	14	5
6	13	17	4

a) Put a tick next to the horizontal line that totals 40.

b) Colour the horizontal line that makes the biggest total in yellow.

c) Colour the vertical line that makes the smallest total blue.

⭐ **Challenge**

Make your own number puzzles by completing the grids.

5		
	4	
		1

		3
	6	
2		

Complete the Think Board for each problem and solve it.

1

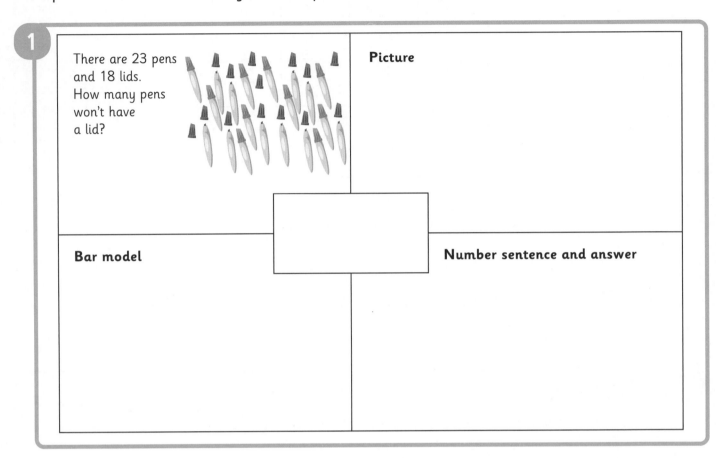

There are 23 pens and 18 lids. How many pens won't have a lid?

Picture

Bar model

Number sentence and answer

2

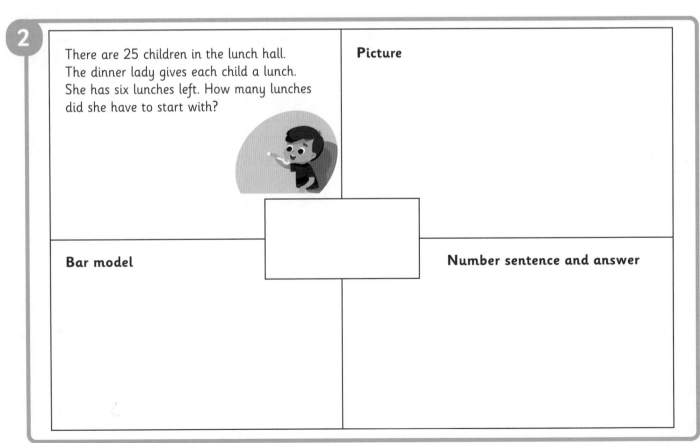

There are 25 children in the lunch hall. The dinner lady gives each child a lunch. She has six lunches left. How many lunches did she have to start with?

Picture

Bar model

Number sentence and answer

3

Isla has 30 dolls and some teddies. She has six fewer teddies than dolls. How many teddies does Isla have?

Picture

Bar model

Number sentence and answer

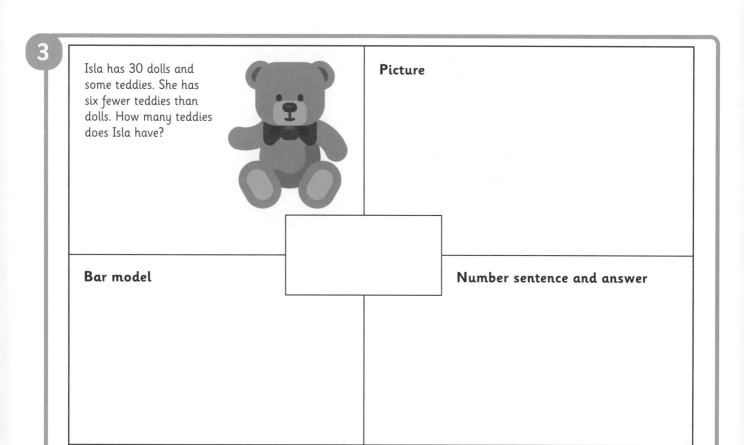

4

There are 23 boys and some girls in Nuria's basketball club. There are seven more girls than boys. How many girls are in the basketball club?

Picture

Bar model

Number sentence and answer

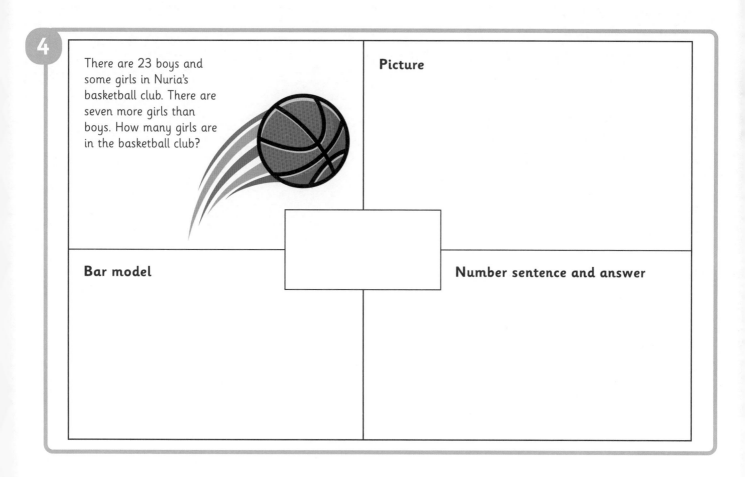

5

Finlay has 35 pairs of red socks and 28 pairs of blue socks. How many more pairs of red socks does Finlay have?

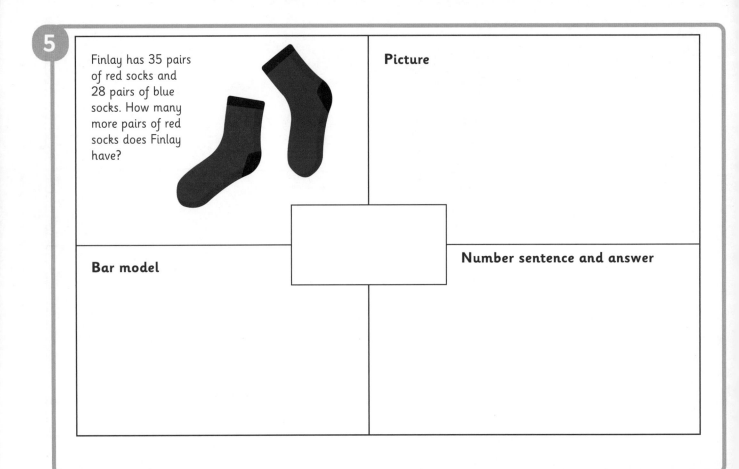

Picture

Bar model

Number sentence and answer

★ **Challenge**

Write two addition number sentences and two subtraction number sentences to fit this bar model.

27	
16	11

Complete the Think Board for each problem and solve it.

1

Amann has 27 pencils. Isla gives him 68 pencils. How many pencils does Amman have now?

Objects, picture or diagram

Bar model

Number line

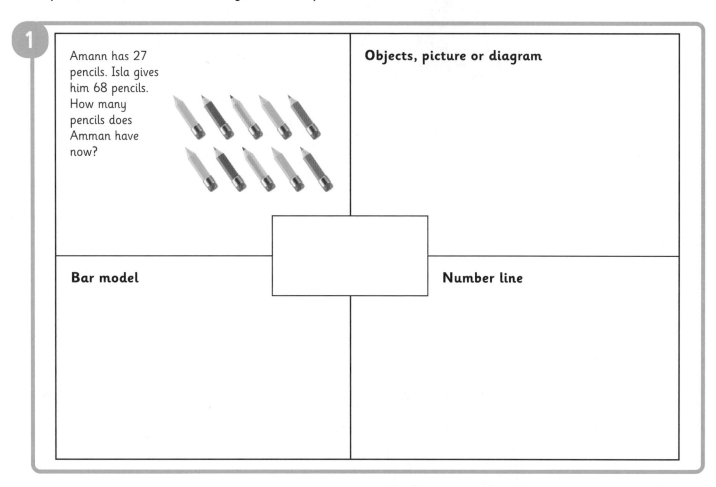

2

Isla scored 46 points on Monday and 59 points on Tuesday. How many more points did Isla score on Tuesday?

Objects, picture or diagram

Bar model

Number line

3

Finlay sold 58 packets of sweets at the school fair. There were 19 left at the end of the fair. How many packets of sweets did Finlay start with?

Objects, picture or diagram

Bar model

Number line

4

Nuria had 43 daisies. She gave some to Isla. Now she has 14. How many daisies did Nuria give to Isla?

Objects, picture or diagram

Bar model

Number line

5

Isla counts 75 doors on the way to school. 37 of them are black. How many doors are not black?

Objects, picture or diagram

Bar model

Number line

★ **Challenge**

Finlay bought a football strip for £48 and football socks for £14. If he pays with seven £10 notes how much change will he get?

4.1 Multiplying by skip counting

1 a) Skip count in threes. Colour each multiple of 3 on the 100 square.

1	2	3	4	5	6	7	8	9	10
11	12	13	14	15	16	17	18	19	20
21	22	23	24	25	26	27	28	29	30
31	32	33	34	35	36	37	38	39	40
41	42	43	44	45	46	47	48	49	50
51	52	53	54	55	56	57	58	59	60
61	62	63	64	65	66	67	68	69	70
71	72	73	74	75	76	77	78	79	80
81	82	83	84	85	86	87	88	89	90
91	92	93	94	95	96	97	98	99	100

b) Write down the next six multiples of 3 that come after 99.

2 a) Isla has made cakes for her birthday party. She has five boxes and puts three cakes in each box. How many cakes does Isla have altogether?

Show how you worked it out.

Complete the number sentence:  ☐ × ☐ = ☐

b) Amman has six pencil pots. He puts three pencils in each pot. How many pencils does Amman have?

Show how you worked it out.

Complete the number sentence: ☐ × ☐ = ☐

Use skip counting to solve these problems. Show your working.

a) How many threes are in 39?

b) What is 15 x 3?

1 Write each problem as an addition number sentence then find the total. The first one has been done for you.

a) Finlay's dad planted six rows of carrots. He put five carrots in each row. How many carrots did he plant in total?

$$5 + 5 + 5 + 5 + 5 + 5 = 30$$

b) There are three spiders. Each spider has eight legs. How many legs are there in total?

c) Isla has nine pots. She puts three pencils in each pot.

How many pencils does she have in total?

d) Amman draws five monsters. Each monster has five eyes.

How many eyes are there in total?

e) Each orange has seven segments. Nuria has two oranges.

How many segments are there in total?

f) A farmer had six pens. He puts three sheep in each pen.

How many sheep are there in total?

g) A flower seller has four buckets. He puts ten flowers in each bucket.

How many flowers are there in total?

h) There are ten tables in the classroom. Each table has four legs.

How many legs are there in total?

2 Nuria and Amman have been planting flowers in the garden. Draw an array to help you work out how many flowers there are altogether. The first one has been done for you.

a) Three rows of six blue flowers

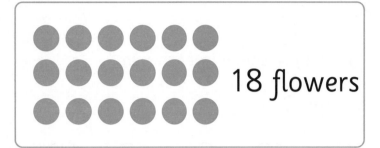

18 flowers

b) Four rows of seven blue flowers

c) Six rows of nine yellow flowers

d) Five rows of eight white flowers

e) Three rows of three purple flowers

f) Two rows of ten pink flowers

★ Challenge

Colour the correct number of squares in the correct number of rows to help solve this problem. 3 x 14 =

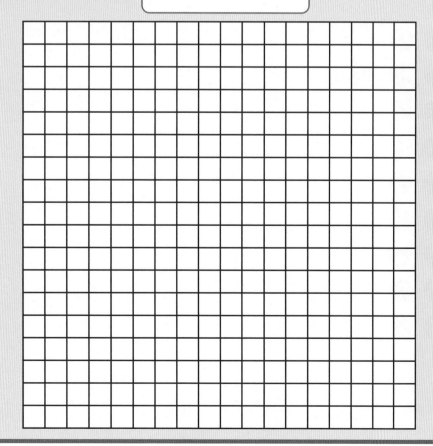

1 Write a multiplication number sentence for each array.

Skip count to work out the answer.

a)

b)

c)

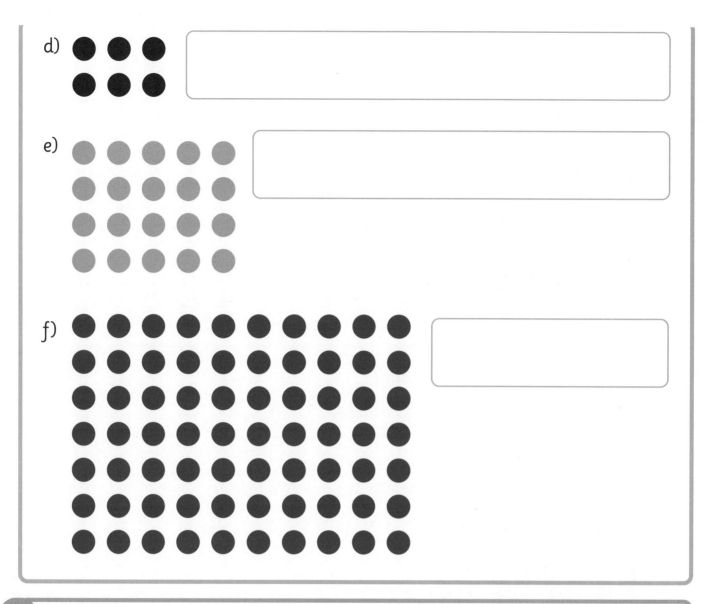

d)

e)

f)

2 Make an array to show each problem, then write a multiplication sentence to match it.

Skip count to work out the answer.

a) Isla has four pizzas for her party. Each pizza has six slices.
How many slices are there altogether?

b) Finlay lines up his toy cars. He makes eight rows of three cars.
How many cars are there altogether?

c) Amman has twelve pairs of shoes.
How many shoes does he have altogether?

d) Nuria has nine rows of three playing cards.
How many cards does she have altogether?

How many different arrays can you make using 48 counters?

Write a multiplication sentence for each array you make.

4.4 Repeated addition

1 Use counters to make a copy of each array. Write an addition number sentence for each array you make. One has been done for you.

a) ● ● ● ● ● ● ● ●
   ● ● ● ● ● ● ● ●

$8 + 8 = 16$

b) ● ● ● ● ●
   ● ● ● ● ●
   ● ● ● ● ●

c) ● ● ● ● ● ● ● ● ● ●
   ● ● ● ● ● ● ● ● ● ●
   ● ● ● ● ● ● ● ● ● ●

d) ● ● ● ● ● ●
   ● ● ● ● ● ●

e) ● ● ● ● ● ●
   ● ● ● ● ● ●
   ● ● ● ● ● ●

2 What adding facts do you know that can help you with these problems? Write down the adding facts you used. You could draw an array to help you.

a) There are five trees, and each tree has five apples on it. How many apples are there altogether?

$5 + 5 + 5 + 5 + 5 = 25$

b) There are three flowers, and each flower has ten petals. How many petals are there altogether?

c) There are five cars and each car has four tyres. How many tyres are there altogether?

d) There are ten trees and each tree has three apples on it. How many apples are there altogether?

Work out the answer to 6 x 5 = [   ]

Can you use your answer to help you solve these problems? Show how you worked each problem out.

a) 5 x 6 =

b) 6 x 6 =

c) 16 x 6 =

1 Write a doubles or tens fact, and a multiplication number sentence, for each array. One has been done for you.

a)

Double 3 = 6   2 x 3 = 6

b)

c)

d)

e)

2 Nuria has made cupcakes. She puts ten in each box.

How many cupcakes has she made? Write your answer as a multiplication number sentence.

a) 5 boxes of 10

b) 7 boxes of 10

c) 8 boxes of 10

d) 10 boxes of 10

3 Finlay is making up bags of sweets for his party. He puts five sweets in each bag.

How many sweets does he have? Write your answer as a multiplication number sentence.

a) 10 bags of 5

b) 3 bags of 5

c) 5 bags of 5

d) 7 bags of 5

e) 8 bags of 5

f) 6 bags of 5

a) Match the double to the multiplication sentence to the answer by drawing lines. One has been done for you.

b) Oh no! The puzzle is incomplete. Write in the missing multiplications sentences and answers.

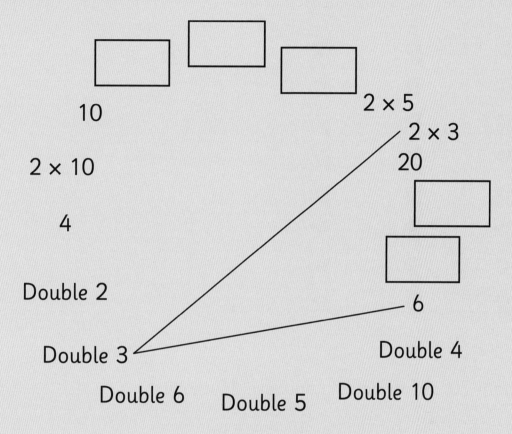

10

2 × 5

2 × 3

2 × 10

20

4

Double 2

6

Double 3

Double 4

Double 6   Double 5   Double 10

c) Make up your own multiplication number puzzle.

4.6 Dividing by sharing

1 Use cubes or counters to help you work out these problems.

a) Share 24 slices of pizza equally between 8 children.

How many slices will each child get?

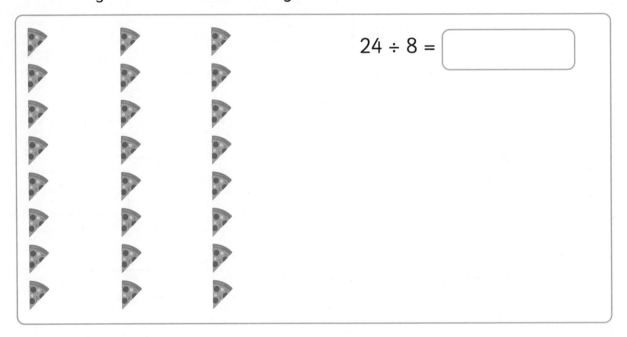

$24 \div 8 =$ ☐

b) Share 70 carrots equally between 10 rabbits.

How many carrots will each rabbit get?

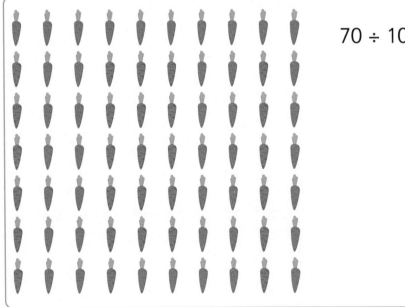

$70 \div 10 =$ ☐

c) Share 15 pieces of chocolate equally between 3 children. How many pieces of chocolate will each child get?

$$15 \div 3 = \boxed{}$$

d) Share 42 apples equally between 6 crates. How many apples will there be in each crate?

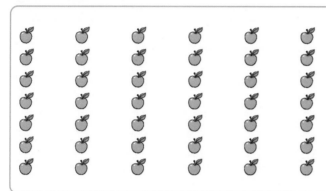

$$42 \div 6 = \boxed{}$$

e) Share 21 treats between 3 dogs. How many treats will each dog get?

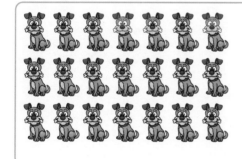

$$21 \div 3 = \boxed{}$$

f) Share 25 fish equally between 5 fish tanks. How many fish will there be in each tank?

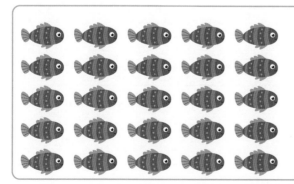

$$25 \div 5 = \boxed{}$$

2 Isla is sharing pens equally between the tables in her classroom.

How many pens will each table get?

Write each answer as a division number sentence.

a) 18 pens and 2 tables

b) 18 pens and 6 tables

c) 30 pens and 6 tables

d) 30 pens and 5 tables

e) 16 pens and 4 tables

f) 32 pens and 4 tables

Draw an array to help you work out the answers to these problems.

a) | 36 divided by 6 =

b) | 36 divided by 9 =

1 Amman's mum and dad are boxing up food in their shop.

Can you work out how many boxes they will need by skip counting?

a) There are 30 bananas and 10 can go in each box.

How many boxes will they need?

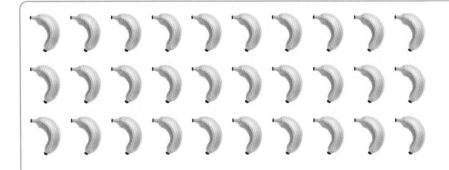

b) There are 24 tins of beans with 4 in each box.

How many boxes did they need?

c) There are 24 loaves of bread with 3 in each box.

How many boxes did they need?

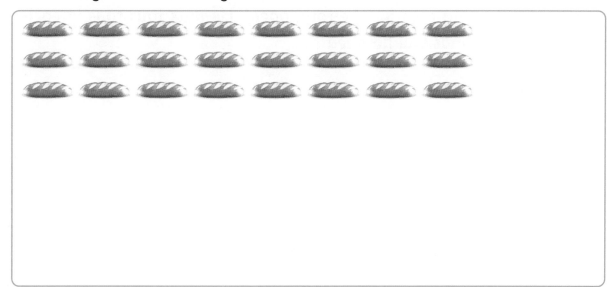

d) There are 35 boxes of cereal with 5 in each box.

How many boxes did they need?

2 Write each answer as a division number sentence. You could use objects or drawings to help you.

Amman is collecting toys for the toy appeal. He puts four toys in each bag. How many bags will he need for:

a) 16 toys

b) 20 toys

c) 28 toys

Isla has 80 buttons. How many different ways can you find to sort these into equal groups? One has been done for you.

10 groups of 8 = 80

4.8 Multiplying by 10

1 Use cubes or base 10 blocks to work out:

a) 3 x 10 = ☐

b) 5 x 10 = ☐

c) 7 x 10 = ☐

d) 6 x 10 = ☐

e) 10 x 10 = ☐

f) 11 x 10 = ☐

2 Write a multiplication number sentence for each array.

a)

☐

b)

☐

c)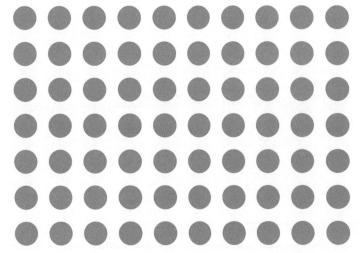

☐

d)

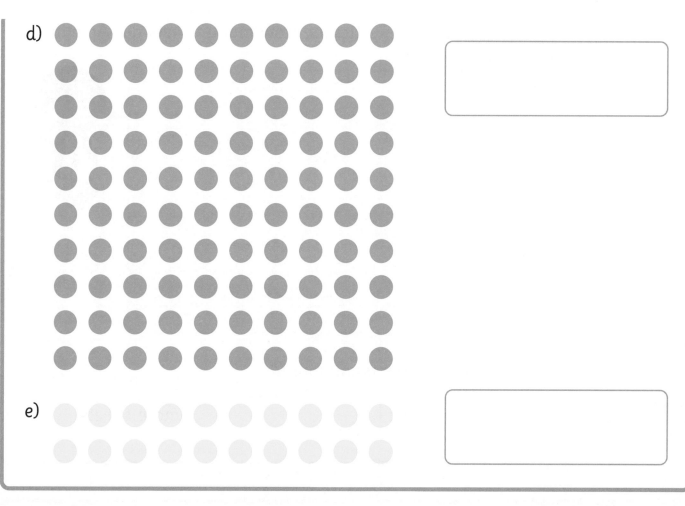

e)

3 a) Nuria sold 150 raffle tickets. Tickets come in bundles of 10. How many bundles of tickets did Nuria sell? Draw an array to help you.

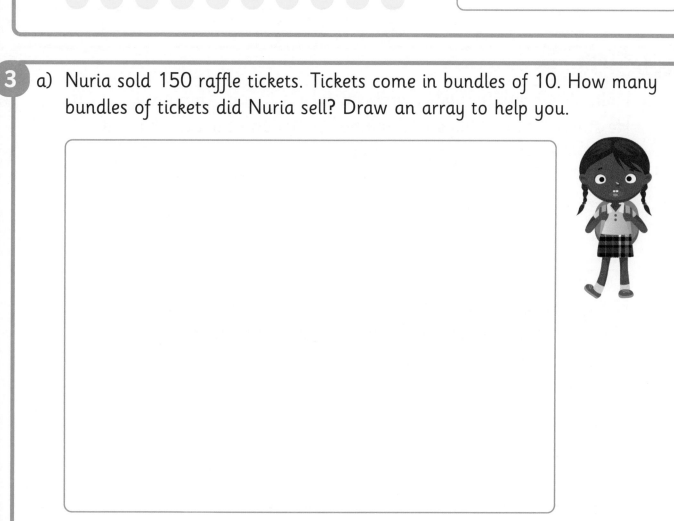

b) Amman sold 12 bundles of 10 tickets. How many tickets did Amman sell? Draw an array to help you.

c) Who sold more tickets? How many more?

[＿＿＿＿＿] sold [＿＿＿＿＿] more tickets.

★ Challenge

a) Finlay is writing a number problem for his friend. The answer is 160. He started by multiplying a number by 10 and then doubling it. What number did Finlay start with?

b) Nuria is writing a number problem for her friend. The answer is 200. She started by multiplying a number by 10 and then doubling it. What number did Nuria start with?

1 Group counters or other objects into tens to help you solve these number problems.

a) 30 ÷ 10 =

b) 60 ÷ 10 =

c) 40 ÷ 10 =

d) 20 ÷ 10 =

e) 10 ÷ 10 =

f) 100 ÷ 10 =

2 How many tens are there in each group of cubes? Write a division number sentence to show your answer.

a)

b)

c)

d)

e)

★ **Challenge**

a) Finlay is collecting stickers. Stickers come in packs of 10. How many packs does he need to buy to give him 70 stickers in total?

Show how you worked it out.

b) Finlay would like to have 200 stickers altogether. How many more packs does he need to buy?

Show how you worked it out.